PORTRAIT OF THE DOG
AS A YOUNG ARTIST

F. BOWMAN HASTIE III

SASQUATCH BOOKS
SEATTLE

Printed in Singapore
  by Star Standard Industries Pte Ltd.

Published by Sasquatch Books

Distributed by Publishers
  Group West

15 14 13 12 11 10 09 08 07 06
9 8 7 6 5 4 3 2 1

COVER PHOTOGRAPHS
Tillie: Dirk Westphal
Frame: C Squared Studios/Photodisc
  Green/Getty Images

COVER + INTERIOR DESIGN
Lesley Feldman

Library of Congress
Cataloging-in-Publication Data
is available.

ISBN 1-57061-464-4

SASQUATCH BOOKS

119 South Main Street
Suite 400
Seattle, Washington 98104
206.467.4300

www.sasquatchbooks.com
custserv@sasquatchbooks.com

THANKS

To my parents, for helping me
appreciate the unexpected and unusual
beauty that springs from life
in so many forms.

To my sister Amelie, for her endless
encouragement and editorial support.

To my brother Matt, for convincing
me not to name my dog Baby Swiss.

To Heidi Lenze, for bringing
Tillie and me to the attention of
Sasquatch Books.

To my agent Simon Green, for
believing in me and in the power
of Tillie.

To Dirk Westphal and Albert
Delamour, for the wonderful photos.

To Stephen Fuller, for all his support
—photographic and otherwise.

To all the people—artists, collectors,
curators, dealers, designers, editors,
friends, television producers and
presenters, Tillie zealots, and other
writers, too numerous to mention by
name—who have contributed to
the success of Tillamook Cheddar.

DEDICATION

TO FLUFFY, TAFFY, AND MERCEDES,
THE BEST FRIENDS OF MY CHILDHOOD,
AND TO MOM, MY BIGGEST SUPPORTER
AND TILLIE'S GREATEST PATRON.

Contents

INTRODUCTION

I was sitting on my couch one day when Tillie was about five months old. I was writing on a yellow legal pad that rested on my lap. All of a sudden, Tillie clambered up beside me, ascended my lap, and began scratching at the very page I was writing on.

I interpreted her act as some attempt at expression. I couldn't imagine she shared my impulse to write. Perhaps she wanted to draw or make an imprint of some kind. Whatever it was, I sensed that she wanted to "mark," though not in the usual way of dogs. But she lacked the means to do so—or, rather, I lacked the means to see her markings. Then I had an idea: I could record her efforts using carbon paper.

Luckily, I had a package of carbon paper in my home office. I quickly fetched a sheet and slipped it under the first blank page of the tablet, figuring that she would tear the carbon paper with her tiny claws if not for a piece of insulation in between. I returned to the couch and held out the prepared pad. Tillie resumed her scratching. With a digging motion, she worked intently at the page. The paper and carbon obscured the image developing beneath, so I couldn't monitor the work in progress. But when she took a break from her markings, I lifted the sheet to reveal her work.

I was impressed by how fully she had saturated the page, using only her tiny puppy claws, with the pigment from the carbon paper. Equally fascinating was the notion of a tangible—and in my mind, beautiful—image resulting from my dog's efforts. It was a product of her work.

Today, I work for Tillie. I am her assistant, her advocate, her chauffeur, and her archivist, to name a few of my duties. I maintain a library that includes her extensive and various media coverage: in print (*PARADE* magazine [Best New Artist, 2004], *The National Examiner*), on radio (NPR, BBC Radio, and *Radio of the Basque Country*), and on television (local TV news and cable-access programs; national and specialty programs such as *Good Morning America, Dogs with Jobs, Animal Magnetism,* and *K9 Karma*; as well as international programs on CNN, TV Tokyo, Telemundo, and Korean Television). The dog's résumé goes on and on. Nearly every clip has featured some variation of the genesis tale above.

Tillie's first artistic work on paper required some simple office supplies, my assistance, and her own will and determination. Her subsequent rise in the art world, however, has depended on a great deal more. ♥

TILLIE

Derek Buckner, 2004
Oil on wood
12 x 12 inches
Collection of
  Tillamook Cheddar

PART ONE:
AN ARTIST IS BORN

TILLIE'S FIRST
FAMILY

Tillamook Cheddar—a.k.a. Tillie—came into the world on January 17, 1999, one of six puppies born to Briarpatch Winnie and Nadua Nitro. It was their first litter. I met the parents and their progeny three weeks later at Kress Country Farms in Greenwich, Connecticut, during my search for a Jack Russell terrier puppy.

I selected Tillie, not based on any indication of artistic prowess, but because she happened to be the last puppy I played with that day. She had fallen asleep in my lap, and breeder Sharon Kress had returned the other pups and their parents to the whelping pad. While we sat down to chat about the challenges and responsibilities of raising a Jack Russell, tiny Tillie dozed peacefully in my arms. Kress warned me about the high energy levels of these dogs, their

demands for attention, and their supreme intelligence, which can lead Jack Russells to train their humans unless authority is established in the opposite direction.

She echoed many of the unofficial disclaimers that accompany the breed: They're bad with children, more likely to "correct" misbehavior than to tolerate it; if not leashed, they may take off after "prey" at any moment, without warning or the promise of return; bred as working dogs, they expect and need to have a "job"—if you do not assign them duties, they will create their own little chores, such as destroying your home. I had come across most of these same warnings in books and on Web sites about the breed. My favorite description was "little thugs in white clown costumes."

I had already ignored most signs that pointed against acquiring a Jack Russell terrier. I was too taken with their winning personalities and overwhelming cuteness to seriously consider all the negative spin, often wielded by breeders to eliminate the weak from the ranks of would-be Jack Russell terrier people. Besides, I couldn't imagine a little dog being capable of bossing me around.

OPPOSITE: Tillie in Williamsburg, 1999. **ABOVE:** Tillie in SoHo, 1999.

Once I convinced the breeder that I could handle a Jack Russell, and wrote her a check for half the amount of a puppy's price tag, she asked me if there was a particular one I wanted. All six littermates were so appealing, I would have been happy to take any one of them home. My ultimate choice of Tillie felt like a mutual decision between me and the adorable creature asleep in my arms. I glanced down: "If this one is available, I'll take her."

Kress described Tillie's parents, Winnie and Nitro, as "exceptional dogs": "Winnie has done everything from achieving success in the show ring and racing, to hunting in the field, to going into psychiatric hospitals and surgical wards as a therapy dog. Nitro is the happiest and friendliest dog around. He too has been successful in the show ring, racing, and hunting in the field. But what he likes most of all is to give and receive lots of lovin'. Everyone who meets Tillie's parents is amazed at their wonderful personalities."

Tillie's siblings have followed in the steps of their parents and achieved similar successes in their dogly endeavors. But Kress noticed early on that the future artist was different from her littermates. "Tillie stood out in the way she would look at you," she recalled. "It was as if she could understand what I was saying. Her look was intent and inquisitive. She was very focused on everything."

TILLAMOOK CHEDDAR:
WHAT'S IN A NAME?

For as long as I can remember, I've always been extremely fond of cheese. When it came time to name my dog, I wanted to give her a cheesy moniker. Two primary contenders were Cambozola and Baby Swiss. "Cammie," "Camby," and "Zola" didn't quite fit, however. And my brother, Matt, warned me against Baby Swiss. "Think about it," he cautioned, "you don't want to be out in public yelling, 'Baby! Baby!' all the time at your dog." I had to concede the point.

I consulted my sister, Amelie, who had always named the family dogs when we were kids. Well, Fluffy and Mercedes, anyway. Amelie suggested Cheddar. Tillamook came to mind because Tillamook Cheddar was the cheese we had grown up eating. It was a mouthful, but shortening it to "Tillie" resulted in a cute nickname that echoed the pup's mother's name, Winnie. I tried it out around the house, and the name stuck.

Tillie and the author
in Tillamook, Oregon,
1999.

EARLY SIGNS

Six weeks after purchasing her I returned to Greenwich to bring Tillie to her new home in Brooklyn. I was working as a freelance writer and living in Williamsburg, a haven for the hipsteratti. I had never been to art school, but I had plenty of artists for friends; Williamsburg often felt like an art-school town without the art school. Perhaps this expressive environment led Tillie toward her creative en-deavors. Or maybe her innate artistry would have surfaced wherever we lived.

Tillie's first remarkable act of creation occurred before she ever left the house. Like all puppies, she required a series of vaccinations before being allowed in the outside world. So for her first few weeks in Brooklyn she remained primarily in my small apartment. She slept in her crate at night and was confined inside it whenever I left the house. During this initial house-training period, I encouraged her to do her business on newspapers laid out on the kitchen floor.

One afternoon I awoke from a nap to find a surprise. Tillie had had the run of the house during my daytime slumber and had left a curious turd on the kitchen floor—not on the *New York Times* business section but on the bare linoleum beside it. At first

I was disappointed that she had missed the mark, but when I looked closer, my chagrin turned to amazement.

Tillie's "accident" carried a shocking form. The unmistakable shape of a man—flat on his back, with a round head, defined facial features, torso, two legs spread slightly apart, and two arms, extending into hands clasped on the Poop Man's lap—lay on the floor. I was never one to take photos of feces—before or since the Poop Man miracle—but in this instance I felt compelled to record it. Despite this first serious attempt at sculpture, I did not foresee the forays into art that would follow.

The photograph of Poop Man happened to coincide with Tillie's own first modeling stint, which wasn't exactly a paid gig. The photo session, with New York artist Dirk Westphal, was my idea. I wanted to capture Tillie's irresistible puppiness on film, and I had in mind an annual photo session that would serve as a photographic record of my dog's life.

A fine friend and a great artist, Westphal was an obvious choice for the shoot. His various photographic series—New York City payphones, reconfigured snack cakes, goldfish, mouthwash, and

HUMBLE BEGINNINGS: Soon after Poop Man, Tillie scratched out her first painting.

cough syrup—convey a keen eye for elusive beauty,
a meticulous sense of precision, an unflagging pa-
tience, and a whimsical mind open to the unexpected.
And his fondness for dogs was no secret. As one
of Tillie's earliest babysitters, with a firm hand for
discipline and a soft spot for puppies, Westphal had
already earned her admiration, love, and respect.
The feelings were clearly mutual. As a photo subject,
Tillie further impressed him. "Even though she was
just a couple of months old," Westphal remembered,
"she already had what seemed like a practiced
professionalism about her. She was very responsive,
both to me and to the camera."

UNTITLED NO. 1

Tillamook Cheddar, 1999
Carbon on paper
8.5 x 14 inches
Collection of the Artist

NO DOGS ALLOWED INSIDE:

Tillie at the Metropolitan
Museum of Art, 2004.

PART TWO:
TILLIE AT WORK

EXHIBITIONS +
INSTALLATIONS

Tillie's early interest in working with paper (as discussed in the introduction of this book), combined with my willingness to indulge her endeavors, quickly led to the blossoming of a bona fide art career. Beginning when she was still a puppy, and continuing beyond the birth of her own puppies, Tillie has compiled an exhibition record that has many human artists snarling with jealousy. As her materials have evolved along with her technique, Tillie's ascent has been bolstered by the combination of fortuitous social contacts, her natural affinity with other artists, the courage of a select few curators and dealers, prodigious media coverage, and an expanding popular fascination with her accomplishments.

-Dog Tag-

After Tillie created her original work on paper, I assisted her in a similar manner for a couple more drawings on the same yellow pad. From there I began taping carbon paper—again with an insulating piece of paper on top—to sheets of plain white paper on the wood floors of our apartment. At first I felt silly, acting as a studio assistant to my dog. But Tillie expressed an unbridled enthusiasm for the process, and I was already cultivating a genuine aesthetic appreciation for her works.

Taping the paper to the floor relieved me from having to hold the tablet while Tillie worked. It also provided the budding young artist with more freedom in approaching her "canvas." She created a series of works in this fashion, which I proudly shared with some of my artist friends, including Larry Pickens, who was about to open a new gallery in his Williamsburg living space. Upon seeing the work, he invited Tillie to be the inaugural artist at his teethovenstudio. Tillie and I set about preparing works for an October showing, to be titled -Dog Tag-. At a Manhattan art-supply store I found a type of color-transfer paper that functioned like carbon paper and was available in large sheets of five assorted colors—black, white, yellow, blue, and red. I began taping the sheets to pieces of mat board, which allowed Tillie to move the pieces about while she was working, freeing her from the anchor of paper taped to the floor and allowing her to work on bigger canvases.

Using a combination of tooth and claw, Tillie produced more than sixty works for her first exhibition. I invited my friend Sean Flaherty, a poet, to help me name them. Among my favorite titles were "Voodoo Massai," "Tip O'Neil," "Kite Flying in China," "Burger King 1976," and "The Rauschenberg." Another friend, the artist Ravi Rajakumar, produced a video documenting Tillie's creation of

FASHION BRUT: Tillie posing in Burberry at Green Gallery during Art Brut exhibition, Williamsburg.

two early works. Those who attended the opening were able to view "Tillamook Cheddar: Artist in Action" on a video monitor in the gallery.

Proceeds from the sales were to benefit the Brooklyn Animal Resource Coalition (BARC), a local shelter, but honestly I did not expect there to be any sales. I had taken the necessary leap of faith to believe in my dog as an artist, but I doubted the art-buying public — whatever that was — would join me. Luckily, I was wrong: Tillie's first collector was a dog.

As soon as Tillie received all of her puppy vaccinations, I began walking her each morning to McCaren Park. A scruffy patch of grass was designated for the dogs of Williamsburg to run around off-leash, while their artsy humans engaged their pets in play

or chatted among themselves. Tillie's first friend at the park was a likable hound named Nelson. They were nearly identical in age, and although Tillie was significantly smaller, they loved to rough it up together. Naturally I invited Nelson to Tillie's opening, along with his humans, Cheryl and Mo Willems. And I'm glad I did. On Nelson's behalf they purchased a small yellow and black piece titled "Circus Life (Cedric Meet My Monkey)." It was nine-month-old Tillie's first sale.

Perhaps as significant as this first sale was another transaction made at the teethovenstudio opening. The artist Tom Sachs, another friend of mine and Tillie's, agreed to trade one of his small Hello Kitty sculptures for an undisclosed number of Tillie's paintings. And so began Tillie's own private art collection.

1999 WORK

**CIRCUS LIFE
(CEDRIC MEET MY MONKEY)**

Tillamook Cheddar, 1999
Color transfer on foamcore
10 x 9 inches
Collection of Nelson
  Willems

THERE'S A
CHAINSAW COMING

Tillamook Cheddar, 1999
Color transfer on mat
22 x 28 inches
Collection of the Artist

SOMBRERO SLALOM
(right)

Tillamook Cheddar, 1999
Color transfer on mat
28 x 22 inches
Collection of the Artist

LADY IN RED: Dirk Westphal's Tillie on red, SoHo, 2000.

Portraits + Landscapes

Around the time of Tillie's first exhibition, we were forced out of our Williamsburg apartment. "No dogs allowed" was the reason our landlord, George, gave. Lucky for us, though, the grass was greener on the other side of Brooklyn; for one thing, there was grass. Our new place in Prospect Heights turned out to be perfect, offering a backyard, plenty of space for Tillie's new studio, seemingly understanding landlords, and close proximity to Prospect Park, a veritable heaven-on-earth for dogs.

The park's sprawling half-mile expanse of green —known as the Long Meadow—functions as a morning and evening dog run deluxe. Dogs can range off-leash and unencumbered by fences everyday before 9 a.m. and after 9 p.m. On week-end mornings the number of four-legged frolickers reaches well into the hundreds. The dogs cavort with their humans as if inhabitants of a planet where people and animals live as near equals, with the animals maintaining a slight advantage.

Some dog-person duos roam independently, others in small packs. Sticks, balls, Frisbees, and favorite dog toys are tossed, caught, flung, and retrieved. Inevitable cliques gather in various clusters, some eclectic and others exclusive according to breed. We learned to steer clear of Poodle Town and Ridgeback Hill, instead favoring Valley of the Pugs and shady Squirrel Grove. Tillie's new romping grounds made her old stomping grounds of McCar-ren Park seem like a hardscrabble prison yard in comparison. In the Long Meadow, Tillie discovered two new passions: playing ball and chasing squir-rels. Happy in our new Brooklyn setting, Tillie's capacities for work and play bristled with new life.

Soon Tillie's paintings would receive a new injection of color. Walking by a neighborhood frame shop a few weeks after our move, I wondered if the propri-etors might have some spare pieces of mat board they would be willing to donate to a young up-and-coming artist. Once I introduced Tillie, the folks at San Art Framing and Supplies were happy to provide us with all the leftover mat pieces we could carry home. Lengths and widths of the pieces ranged from a few inches to more than two feet, and they came in a vast array of colors: earth tones, greens, yellows, blues, pinks and purples, and many shades of white, in addition to the solid blacks.

The thickness, texture, and rectangular shape and size of each board also varied, opening up new realms for Tillie's work. Combining the color-transfer paper with contrasting pieces of mat board led Tillie to create a new series of works. Again I recruited Flaherty to help name the pieces, with a focus on person and place. The portrait sub-jects, as determined by Flaherty, included Damien Hirst, Courtney Love, Ronald Reagan, Bootsy Collins, and Udo Kier. Landscape paintings carried such titles as "Never Been to Texas," "3-mile Island," "Prospect Park II," and "I Went to the Beach Twice."

In the spring of 2000, I brought Tillie back to West-phal for her second annual photo session. Compared with the cute puppy photos of the year before, the new series, featuring Tillie posed dramatically before a red backdrop, revealed a more mature animal, self-assured and beautiful. We followed up the studio session with a special outdoor shoot at Prospect Park, where Westphal snapped a series of action photos with Tillie leaping for her beloved blue ball. He also took some memorable shots of Tillie sprawled out in the green grass of the Long Meadow.

The *Portraits and Landscapes* exhibit opened at 105 Devoe, another small gallery in Williamsburg, on October 21, 2000. In addition to forty-two portraits and landscapes—of which nearly all were sold by the close of the show—the exhibit also featured a series of miniature spiral-bound books, which Tillie had recently completed by creating tiny original drawings on each page, as well as a number of new sculptural works.

3-D Tillie: More Forays into Sculptural Form

Tillie had begun working with golf balls the previous winter during a visit to the Oregon Coast, where my mother has a beach house at Arch Cape, about forty miles north of the Tillamook County Creamery Association (creators of the famed Tillamook Cheddar, Tillie's namesake). At first I considered the golf balls Tillie found on the beach to be mere toys. She'd excitedly bring one to me and drop it at my feet, barking insistently for me to throw it. After chasing the ball across the sand, she would crouch down and furiously chew at it for a few minutes while I continued walking down the beach. Eventually she'd catch up and return the ball for another throw.

The golf balls emerged as a sculptural medium when I realized the degree to which Tillie was able to mutate their uniform surface with her teeth. Through deliberate biting and chewing, she was able to alter the very nature of the thing. What began as a human-engineered, highly regular, machine-tooled, symmetrical, smoothly dimpled spherical surface became a jagged, pock-marked, thoroughly individualized outer covering of the same basic sphere—no longer suitable for golf or any other recognized sport, except perhaps fetch. Tillie was able to affect the essential decomposition of the golf ball using the most basic tool—her own teeth. In this manner the artist was able to transform an ordinary, everyday object into something unique and beautiful.

I first considered exhibiting these deconstructed golf balls during a visit to the driving range at New York City's Chelsea Piers in the summer of 2000. At the time the driving range was sponsored in part by Urban Fetch, a short-lived Internet-based delivery service. I noticed that each golf ball at the driving range had been imprinted with the Urban Fetch logo, making them a perfect medium for a city-dwelling dog-artist like Tillamook Cheddar. I acquired a modest supply of the imprinted balls and presented them to Tillie as new material for her sculptural work. She needed no further direction before starting in on the balls. Eight of the newly modified balls were presented at 105 Devoe as the "Urban Fetch series," displayed on a shelf below another dramatic sculptural series of Tillie's, "Where's Your Baby's Face?"

FETCHING ART: Aside from her paintings, Tillie also dabbles with sculptural works.

"Where's Your Baby's Face?" is a set of four identical latex chew toys standing at various stages
of decomposition, each one surgically altered by the
artist using her paws and teeth. The toys were orig-
inally in the shape of miniature dogs, actually three-
dimensional models of the Big Dogs Sportswear
company logo. Although they are meant to represent
a Saint Bernard, the little "Big Dogs" in their original form bear a striking resemblance to Tillie: their
bodies are predominantly white, and black patches
mark their faces on each side.

LOBOTOMY (DOC ELLIS)

Tillamook Cheddar, 2000
Baseball
Collection of the Artist

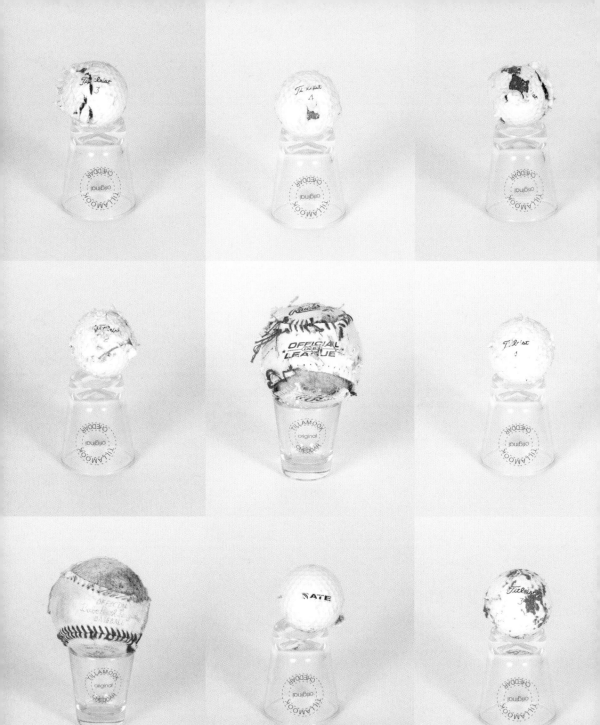

The inspiration for showing "Where's Your Baby's Face?" originated in Tillie's natural affinity for the material. When she got her first little "Big Dog" chew toy, it became an instant object of obsession. Tillie had never encountered a chew toy made of latex before, and it proved to be far more resilient than those made of rubber and other plastics. The toy also resembled Tillie as none of her toys ever had. She took to toting the little dog wherever she went. At the office where I was working at the time, my boss, Joanna Pello—one of Tillie's great admirers and consummate playmates during our stint at her company—began referring to the little dog as Tillie's baby. "Where's your baby?" Pello would ask, if Tillie were ever without her little dog. Tillie would dart off to fetch it, and play would commence.

Tillie typically takes mere minutes to reduce a squeaky rubber hedgehog—or the plastic edition of the *Daily Growl*—to a scattering of bite-size bits. First she renders the toy squeakless, either by removing the plastic whistle or tearing a hole in the object, creating an alternate exit for air. Once the toy is mute, Tillie wastes no time in achieving its thorough deconstruction, holding the object in her paws while decimating it with her teeth.

But it took Tillie weeks to penetrate the surface of her beloved "baby." She first broke through at the nose, removing the tip of the dog's snout, wagging tongue and all. Surprisingly, she maintained her latex pup in this anonymous condition for an additional few weeks, before dismantling its entire head and working down its torso. During this period of decomposition my coworkers and I began playfully asking Tillie, "Where's your baby's face?"

During the *Portraits and Landscapes* exhibition, Tillie discovered yet another sculptural medium when she found an old baseball in the garden outside the gallery. She brought the ball inside and set about deconstructing it, putting her time to good use as we tended the exhibit on a Saturday afternoon. The sculptor Jon Kessler, then chair of the Visual Arts Division of Columbia University's School of the Arts, had heard about the exhibition from gallery director Jana Ragsdale, then a dean at Columbia. Kessler happened to stop by the gallery that day with a group of students. When he saw Tillie on the floor, working on her newfound baseball—gnawing through the red seams and chewing away the distressed leather sheath to expose the outer core of tightly wound string—Kessler remarked, "Entire careers have been based on less than that."

I purchased a dozen baseballs for Tillie, and we included a number of the resulting sculptures in her next show.

THE ARTIST AT WORK: Tillie digs into "Prominent Nose," SoHo.

Merkin

David Selig, a restaurateur with a gallery connected to his floor of offices in SoHo, was showing an exhibition of photographs by Dirk Westphal when Westphal introduced us in the fall of 2000. In the art world, where dogs eat dogs, Westphal took a different approach and suggested a show of Tillie's works to follow his exhibition at Selig's gallery on Grand Street. *Merkin* opened at 176 Grand on December 7, two weeks after the close of *Portraits and Landscapes.* To promote the show, Selig took out a full-page ad in *Artforum* that featured Westphal's classic Tillie-on-red profile shot.

The exhibition was another unmitigated success. Artist Tom Sachs added to his collection of Tillamook Cheddars by purchasing Tillie's "Furry Brancusi." Other art-world luminaries in attendance were the painters Damien Loeb and Mark Kostabi. I heard that art-rocker/animal activist Moby also showed up, but I didn't see him and he didn't purchase a piece. A dozen new collectors did, however, including the actress Martha Plimpton.

Soon after the exhibition ended, Tillie commemorated her conquest of the city in two more photo sessions with Westphal. An outdoor shoot captured a precocious Tillie in snowy Central Park, with a partial Manhattan skyline behind her. Back at Westphal's studio, which happened to be the site of Tillie's second birthday celebration, he took a series of photos documenting Tillie's creative process.

2000 WORK

MADE IN OREGON
(left)

Tillamook Cheddar, 2000
Color transfer on mat
12 x 12 inches
Collection of the Artist

SNIFFING MONDRIAN

Tillamook Cheddar, 2000
Color transfer on mat
14 x 10 inches
Private Collection

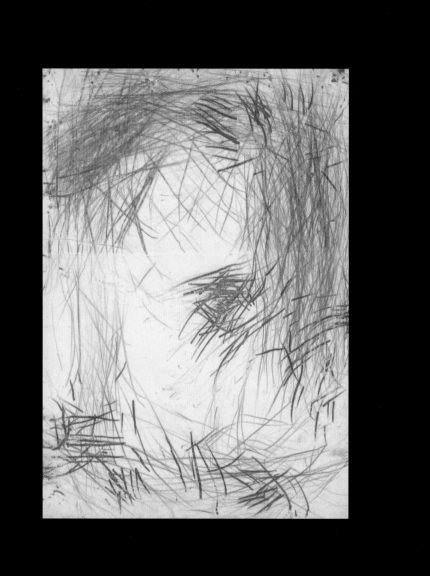

DEAD GIRL
(left)

Tillamook Cheddar, 2000
Color transfer on mat
14 x 11 inches
Collection of the Artist

NEVER BEEN
TO TEXAS
(top)

Tillamook Cheddar, 2000
Color transfer on mat
13 x 13 inches
Collection of the Artist

SUBWAY SERIES
(bottom)

Tillamook Cheddar, 2000
Color transfer on mat
11.5 x 13.5 inches
Collection of the Artist

Goin' to California

After Tillie's successful Manhattan debut, I thought she was ready to take on the Los Angeles art scene. We soon found out, however, that Southern California wasn't completely prepared for Tillie. I had a few friends in LA, and my sister is a professor at the University of California at Santa Cruz. I was overdue for a trip to the Golden State and hoped that Tillie might help pave our way. The plan was to circulate through the LA galleries to drum up some interest in Tillie's work, then head up the coast in our rented convertible. My sister offered to set up a small exhibition, and one of her fellow faculty members, the artist Nobuho Nagasawa, invited us to visit her senior arts seminar.

A chance meeting in New York, on the eve of our departure for the West Coast, struck me as an auspicious send-off. Tillie and I had stopped by Sachs's studio to drop off "Furry Brancusi," the piece he had purchased from the *Merkin* exhibition. We were also meeting Flaherty there to deliver a smaller painting, titled "Merkin," as a reward for his help in naming many of the works in the exhibit as well as the exhibit itself. We were surprised by the arrival at the studio of Gian Enzo Sperone and one of his associates. Neither Tillie nor I had any idea who they were, but Sachs took me aside to inform me that we were about to meet the man who had given Andy Warhol his first exhibition in Europe.

Sachs led us toward them. "Enzo, I want to introduce you to the hottest artist in New York." A dapper man with silver hair, a finely trimmed beard, and beautiful shoes, Sperone locked my eyes and extended his hand. I, of course, gestured toward the terrier at my feet.

When Sperone asked to see Tillie's work, the only pieces at hand were the two I had just delivered to Sachs and Flaherty, who both proved more than happy to part with their new acquisitions. Sperone, one of the foremost art dealers in the world, admired the works and inquired about purchasing "Merkin." A price was agreed upon and he bought the painting—from Flaherty.

Bolstered by our first sale to an important European dealer, we boarded the plane the next day for Los Angeles. Aside from a cute write-up in *LA Weekly* and some overdue visits with good friends, Los Angeles was a bit of a disappointment. The Belgian artist Wim Delvoye would later explain to me that the art world is "100 percent social." It all comes down to who you know and who knows you. Talent, youth, beauty, novelty—even genius—can only get you so far. Well, I didn't know anyone connected to the gallery scene in LA, and neither did Tillie, so we didn't make much headway.

Up in Santa Cruz we presented a small exhibition and a demonstration of Tillie's technique at the My Sister's Kitchen gallery. Coincidentally, the gallery was in my sister's kitchen. Although sales were not exactly brisk, the exhibition, titled *No Dogs On Campus*, did elicit earnest regard and intelligent debate among the professors and their families in attendance—among them art historians, artists, and curators. Faculty and students alike were inspired by Tillie's appearance—one art class, led by Beth Stephens, spent their next session scratching and creating work on the floor.

Debut

Back in New York, Tillie hooked up with Magic Propaganda Mill (MPM), a Brooklyn-based pop art collective founded by Ricardo Cortes, an enterprising firebrand whose various avocations include author, artist, activist, DJ, designer, educator, and publisher. Cortes described his attraction to Tillie as follows: "When it came time to find an artist with her nose in the streets, an artist without pretension but with skills and the strength to carry her own weight, we looked up Tillamook Cheddar."

In July 2001 an exhibition of new works by MPM-affiliated artists, titled *Debut*, opened at the Method Lab gallery in Williamsburg. In addition to a series of mini-diptychs (color transfer on suede mat), Tillie unveiled her largest work ever—the mosaic installation "30-Day Sentence." Correspondent Jeanne Moos covered the event for CNN, affording Tillie her first international television coverage.

Black + White
(And Red, White + Blue)

Most of the new work for Tillie's next solo exhibition—black-and-white color-transfer pieces on paper and suede mat—was already complete when the World Trade Center towers were destroyed on September 11, 2001. Like many other local artists, New Yorkers, and people throughout the United States, Tillie and I got caught up in the patriotic fervor of the times. My friend Eric Lewis, an artist, designer, and *New Yorker* cartoonist, suggested that Tillie do a U.S. flag series in response to the events. I liked the idea and facilitated it by segmenting the color-transfer paper to approximate the color fields of the flag—a blue rectangle in the upper-left corner, with the remainder of the white mat covered in red transfer paper. The resulting pieces struck me as expressionistic abstractions of the American flag, conveying the unique energy and uncertainty that characterized New York City in the weeks following the catastrophe.

I decided to include a group of flags—part of the "Dog Bless America" series—in the exhibition, shown in an alternative gallery space near Times Square. I appended the title *Black + White* to include the parenthetical *And Red, White + Blue*, and donated proceeds from the art sales to a special ASPCA disaster relief fund.

After seeing the flags, another friend, the artist Ryan McGinness, suggested a series of World Trade Center tributes. I helped Tillie achieve a dramatic visual effect by affixing paper to the mat—masking out Twin Tower shapes—before covering the board with transfer paper. We submitted two of these tribute pieces to *Reactions*, an open exhibition at the nonprofit SoHo gallery Exit Art, which gathered the aesthetic responses to the tragedy from hundreds of other artists.

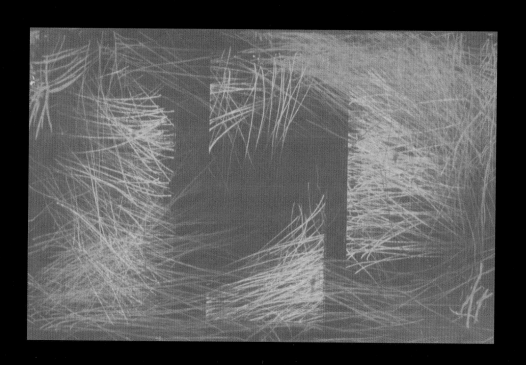

DEFENDER
(left)

Tillamook Cheddar, 2000
Color transfer on suede mat
11 x 17 inches
Collection of the Artist

3-MILE ISLAND

Tillamook Cheddar, 2000
Color transfer on suede mat
11.5 x 18 inches
Collection of the Artist

TIPPER

Tillamook Cheddar, 2000
Color transfer on mat
13.5 x 11 inches
Collection of the Artist

2001 WORK

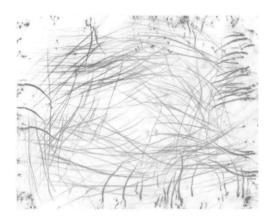

DOG BLESS AMERICA
(BOMBS OVER BAGHDAD)
(left)

Tillamook Cheddar, 2001
Color transfer on suede mat
11 x 14 inches
Private Collection

DOG BLESS AMERICA
(BEN WAS NEVER PREZ,
PART 2)
(top)

Tillamook Cheddar, 2001
Color transfer on suede mat
11 x 14 inches
Collection of Molly Lewis

DOG BLESS AMERICA
(CNN 1)
(middle)

Tillamook Cheddar, 2001
Color transfer on suede mat
11 x 14 inches
Private Collection

DOG BLESS AMERICA
(BEN WAS NEVER PREZ,
PART 1)
(bottom)

Tillamook Cheddar, 2001
Color transfer on suede mat
11 x 14 inches
Collection of Molly Lewis

Collarobations

Tillie's involvement with other artists expanded dramatically over the following months, as she embarked on collaborations with twenty-six different humans. Tillie's interaction with so many experienced contemporaries allowed her to forge new territories, exploring such diverse media as printmaking, sculpture, photography, fresco, audio, and performance. These collaborative endeavors resulted in forty-eight works for the *Collarobations* exhibition. The April 25, 2002, opening drew record crowds to the prestigious National Arts Club and set off another flurry of press coverage. Showcasing successful collaborative works produced by Tillie and such established artists as Diane Dwyer, Jennifer Hoover, Jon Kessler, Andrew Kromelow, Ryan McGinness, Randy Moore, Tom Sachs, Adam Stennett, and Dirk Westphal, the *Collarobations* exhibition raised Tillie's stature to new heights.

Bitch

In the months after *Collarobations* one of Tillie's collaborators, Diane Dwyer, conceived of a performance/video piece for herself and Tillie, titled "BITCH." She also invited Tillie to do a demonstration for the drawing class she taught at the University of Connecticut in Storrs. In September 2002, Tillie and I drove up to the campus to participate in the production of "BITCH" — Tillie's second major video work — and to address the drawing class, our second such appearance. For the classroom demo, Tillie illustrated her technique, and I fielded questions from students. As with our earlier visit to Nagasawa's class at Santa Cruz, the performance came off without a hitch.

The delivery of "BITCH" was not so easy, however. The performance involved Tillie, Dwyer, a four-by-six-foot piece of half-inch Plexiglas, and a wheelbarrow full of topsoil. In a stark white room Dwyer lay on her back, naked, supporting with her hands, legs, and feet the Plexiglas, covered with a layer of soil. The idea was for Tillie to dig away the topsoil, to reveal her collaborator beneath. A second shot — executed from beneath the Plexiglas — showed Tillie digging dirt away from the surface to reveal herself.

The performance presented a unique challenge for both artists. Dwyer's initial feat was one of strength and endurance, as she saddled herself with the prodigious weight of the Plexiglas, the dirt, and a digging dog. Later she would tackle the aesthetic task of editing the video footage. Tillie faced the novel composite of dirt on plastic on woman, in an unfamiliar art-school setting. She had to balance her instincts as a dog and an artist with the utter uncertainty of the situation and its participants' expectations. The result was something of a mutual torment between the artists, which resulted in beautiful still images and an arresting video.

BITCH

Diane Dwyer and
 Tillamook Cheddar, 2002
Video still courtesy
 Diane the American
 Swimmer

2002 WORK

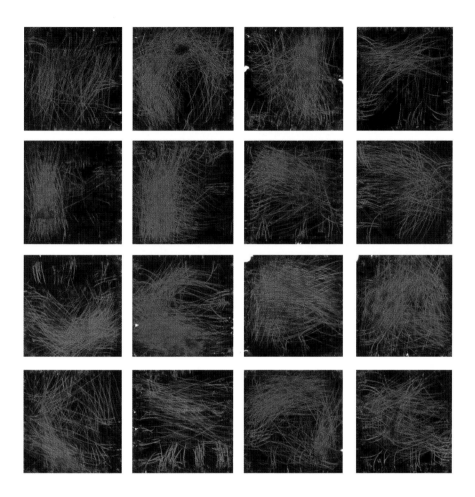

16 ASSASSINS

Tillamook Cheddar, 2002
Color transfer on suede mat
Sixteen 10- x 10-inch panels
Collection of the Artist

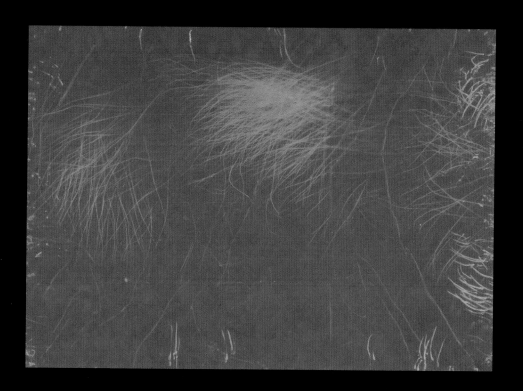

PROMINENT NOSE
(left)

Tillamook Cheddar, 2002
Color transfer on
  suede mat
17 x 11 inches
Private Collection

SPIT-FIRE

Tillamook Cheddar, 2002
Color transfer on suede mat
20 x 28 inches
Collection of Mr. De Smet

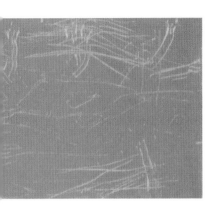

THE ILIAD

Tillamook Cheddar, 2002
Color transfer on mat
Two 11- x 40-inch panels
Private Collection

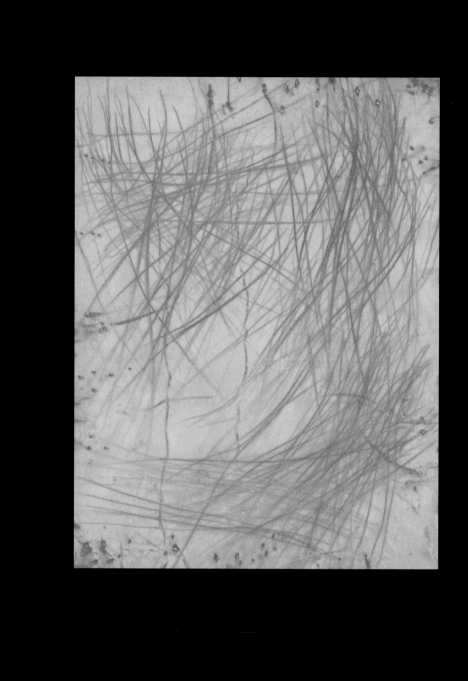

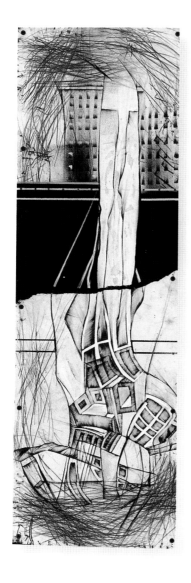

Petropolis

Tillie reached an important milestone in her career in July 2003—her first inclusion in a museum exhibition. *Petropolis: A Social History of Urban Animal Companions*, presented at New York City's oldest museum, the New-York Historical Society, included two of Tillie's paintings, "Gas Mask" and "Tesla," as well as the 1999 Rajakumar video "Tillamook Cheddar: Artist in Action." In an ironic twist that highlighted Tillie's outsider status within the art world, the museum welcomed us to the opening festivities but barred the artist from entering the exhibition, citing insurance restrictions.

On a brighter note, the exhibition afforded us an opportunity to direct some art-world karma back toward our favorite photographer. We referred the *Petropolis* curators to Dirk Westphal, and they enthusiastically included one of his goldfish photos as well as his video "A Work of Art in the Age of Digital Reproduction." Unlike Tillie, Westphal was allowed to view the exhibition in its entirety.

Art Brut

Tillie made two personal connections in 2003 that would profoundly influence the future of her career. First, through her collector and collaborator Tom Sachs, we made the acquaintance of Belgian artist Wim Delvoye. Delvoye's body of work includes heraldic ironing boards, tattooed pigs, Gothic-inflected construction equipment, stained-glass soccer goals, processed-meat mosaics, and fictional cartography. He is perhaps best known for "Cloaca," a room-size machine that simulates the human digestive system—literally converting food into feces—which has been exhibited in museums all over the world. During one of Delvoye's visits to New York,

I facilitated a special demonstration by Tillie of her art technique. Seeing her in action, the Belgian immediately exclaimed: "She is a true artist!"

Many people had already compared Tillie's works with the early scribble-scratch paintings by the American ex-pat Cy Twombly. Upon seeing her finished work unveiled, Delvoye took the comparison a step further, asserting: "It is like Twombly. But much better than Twombly." Delvoye took Tillie under his wing and pledged to find a gallery in Europe to represent her.

Meanwhile, closer to home, Tillie found a new outlet for her art in Brooklyn. Michael Pollack had been directing Green Gallery in Williamsburg for some four years when he finally met Tillie through a mutual friend. Pollack, who now operates the gallery Baden-Powell in Lower Manhattan, recalled his attraction to Tillie: "I needed younger artists, and wanted someone who appealed to the mass audience. The creation of art is an intimidating exercise, yet everybody [upon seeing Tillie's work] believes that *their* canine can do the same thing. Why? I don't know. Because none of them can."

Art Brut opened January 29, 2004, twelve days after Tillie's fifth birthday. The exhibition of sixteen framed oil-on-paper works represented another dramatic injection of color into Tillie's work. On a trip to the art-supply store in the summer of 2003, I found our supplier's inventory of color-transfer paper to be nearly depleted. I was informed that the company that manufactured the paper—a large-format acrylic-wax compound with richness and palate that exceeded our original carbon paper—had gone out of business.

Luckily, the painter Lisa Steiner, who shared her studio with Tillie during the 2003 DUMBO (District Under Manhattan Bridge Overpass) Arts Under

PORTRAIT OF THE ARTIST: Tillie poses with "Prominent Nose."

the Bridge Festival, led us to Robert Doak, who makes paints and pigments in his small DUMBO factory. Doak's Brooklyn headquarters also functions as a modest art-supply store. Intrigued by Tillie's work, he helped me develop a color-transfer technique by applying paint-stick to vellum paper and rolling out a smooth layer of pigment with a brayer (typically used in printmaking). The new materials broke Tillie's palate wide open, as she was no longer confined to the red, yellow, blue, white, and black that had been provided by the now unavailable color-transfer paper.

The colors in *Art Brut* ranged from the brilliant red-orange of "Brooklyn Bridge" to the subtle mauve of "For Japan" to the commingling of orange and green in "Youth & Beauty" and beyond. In addition to the new oil paintings, *Art Brut* included portraits of Tillie—some with the artist alone, some with a pair of stuffed fawns, all against a sharp blue backdrop—taken during the 2003 session with Westphal. Also shown in the exhibition were framed large-format C-prints of the 2002 "Auto-Portraits" produced by Westphal and Tillie for the *Collarobations* exhibit. Based on the show, London's *The Art Newspaper* heralded Tillie as "New York's Hottest New Artist" in a front-page banner.

2003 WORK

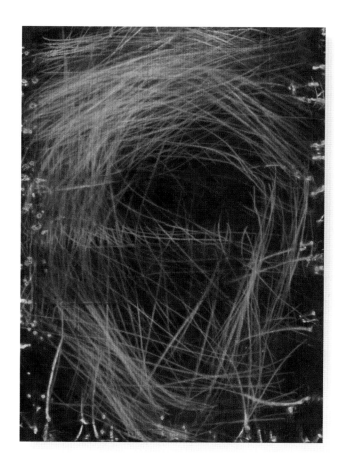

GAS MASK

Tillamook Cheddar, 2003
Color transfer on suede mat
18 x 12 inches
Collection of the Artist

WOMAN
(left)

Tillamook Cheddar, 2003
Color transfer on suede mat
28 x 20 inches
Collection of Wim Delvoye

FOR JAPAN

Tillamook Cheddar, 2003
Oil stick on paper
11 x 14 inches
Collection of the Artist

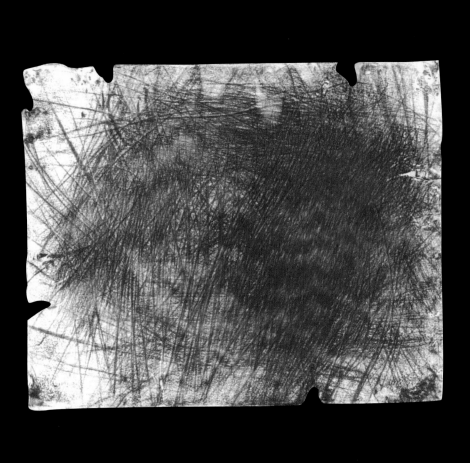

LADY MACBETH
(left)

Tillamook Cheddar, 2003
Oil stick on paper
11 x 14 inches
Collection of Doc Slim Fuller

YOUTH AND BEAUTY
(top)

Tillamook Cheddar, 2003
Oil stick on paper
11 x 14 inches
Collection of the Artist

SOPPING WET
(bottom)

Tillamook Cheddar, 2003
Oil stick and graphite
  on paper
14 x 20 inches
Collection of the Artist

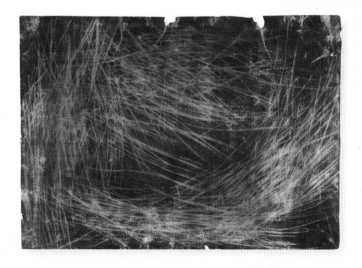

How Are Connected the Displacement and the Machines of Purity

Wim Delvoye's promise came true indeed, and we got a phone call in early 2004 from Jan Hoet Jr., a fellow Belgian who had recently opened Gallery Beaulieu in a seventeenth-century monastery near his hometown of Ghent. Junior, as he prefers to be called, invited Tillie to take part in a two-artist show with Ki Wa, a young painter and performance artist from Estonia. The exhibition, titled *How Are Connected the Displacement and the Machines of Purity*, opened on March 27, 2004. Tillie and I traveled to Belgium the week before, in time to help hang the show and then to join Junior and his partner, Delphine Bekaert, in Milan for the first FlashArt fair.

Tillie's half of the exhibition functioned as an early career retrospective. Along with more than forty paintings—most of them color transfer on mat—we showed a selection of baseballs and golf balls as well as two Cheddar-Westphal "Auto-Portraits." Tillie also performed a public demonstration of her technique at the Sunday afternoon opening, which featured plentiful ham, fresh rolls, and three kinds of soup. The artist did not partake in the copious Belgian beer on offer, but she did take full advantage of the other amenities. She took particular delight in analyzing the ancient scents spread throughout the old building and foraging through the pungent earth of the gallery grounds.

Junior's father, the renowned curator Jan Hoet, founded Ghent's museum of contemporary art, S.M.A.K. We visited the museum one Sunday, and I was pleased to discover that Tillie was granted the same access to the exhibitions as human visitors, although she was required to remain leashed. So we were able to share the pleasure of viewing a painting in the museum's collection by Jan van Imschoot, a local artist who took us to some of the city's essential watering holes during our stay in Ghent.

Tillamook Cheddar: Master in Canine Art

While in Belgium, Tillie and I received an invitation to meet with Ann Demeester, director of the publicly funded arts space W139, in Amsterdam. We spent the final weekend of our European trip touring Amsterdam galleries and museums, visiting the then under construction W139 headquarters and its various temporary outposts. By the time we boarded the train back to Ghent, Tillie and I had agreed to return to Amsterdam for a special exhibition . . . only one month later!

Tillamook Cheddar: Master in Canine Art opened at Kunstvlaai5 on May 8, 2004. The small exhibition of paintings, sculpture, photography, and video was W139's official entry in the sprawling arts festival, a noncommercial counterpart to Amsterdam's annual for-profit art fair, KunstRAI. Tillie's work, and her series of painting demonstrations, drew awe and admiration from the European audience. Touring the other exhibitions and absorbing the work of ascending young artists from Europe and beyond bolstered my faith in the aesthetic value of Tillie's work.

OPPOSITE:
Tillie in SoHo, 2004.

Tillie posing in
one of her
signature T-shirts,
SoHo.

Tillie Ltd.

When Tillie and I returned to Brooklyn we quickly set up shop for a special summer show. Acting on an unwavering commitment to his youngest artist, Pollack designated Green Gallery's project room for a summer installation devoted entirely to Tillie. The "store-in" installation *Tillie Ltd.* opened on June 1, 2004. The first-ever boutique dealing exclusively in the products of a single canine, *Tillie Ltd.* at its inception stocked a full inventory of oil paintings, lithographs, Tillie apparel for dogs and humans, note cards, Tillie totes, and limited-edition cans and bags of Tillie's own brand of dog food.

Tillie's Brooklyn reprise reverberated in Belgium. In July, Gallery Beaulieu staged a solo Tillie show as part of its summer series comprised of ten one-week exhibitions in the coastal city of Knokke-Heist. The momentum of *Tillie Ltd.* carried over into the fall and winter. *Pictures of Tillie*, a special exhibition of portraits by various human artists, opened in *Tillie Ltd.* on September 23, 2004. The store-in remained through the end of the year, when Pollack left the Williamsburg location to found Baden-Powell on Manhattan's Lower East Side. Of course he invited Tillie to come along.

2004 WORK

FEAR OF WATER

Tillamook Cheddar, 2004
Oil stick on paper
16 x 22 inches
Collection of the Artist

PRAYER FIRE
(left)

Tillamook Cheddar, 2004
Oil stick on paper
11.5 x 14.5 inches
Collection of the Artist

THIS WAY
(top)

Tillamook Cheddar, 2004
Oil stick on paper
11 x 14 inches
Collection of the Artist

SATELLITE PHOTO
(bottom)

Tillamook Cheddar, 2004
Oil stick on paper
11.5 x 14.5 inches
Collection of the Artist

WORKING
MOTHER

In 2005 Tillie took a break from exhibitions to embark on a completely new productive phase. While she continued to paint and produce sculpture, perhaps her greatest creations resulted from a collaboration unlike anything Tillie had embarked upon before. For the first time Tillie worked with a fellow canine—a Jack Russell terrier named Eldridge Webster who lived in our neighborhood. While not entirely artistic, their labors were fraught with passion, struggle, pain, and the very essence of life. On July 10, 2005, Tillie gave birth to six healthy, beautiful puppies. Though it's too soon to tell whether any of her offspring will follow their mother toward art careers, it is already clear that motherhood has done little to constrain Tillie's own artistic juggernaut. Even before all of her pups were out the door and headed for new homes, Tillie forged ahead with another exhibition of new works.

On November 2, 2005, one month after being designated "the most successful living animal painter" by the *Art Newspaper* of London, an exhibit of new paintings and limited-edition etchings titled *Afterbirth* opened in SoHo at the Living with Art gallery, operated by Michele Gagne and Albert Delamour. Attending the opening with myself and the artist were three of Tillie's progeny, including the one son who still shares our home—Doc Chinook Strongheart Cheddar. The gallery show coincided with another milestone in Tillie's career. An exhibition of her paintings at the Paterson museum in Paterson, NJ, curated by Baird Jones, was Tillie's first solo exhibition in a museum. It was also the first-ever art exhibition in a museum by a non-human. Features on Tillie soon followed in *The New York Dog* and *Modern Dog* magazines, while her international media coverage extended to German television and *UK Esquire*.

Fortunately none of Tillie's success, fame, or growing fortune has gone to her head. As she continues working and playing, fascinating and amazing, making new friends and creating new art, traveling the continents, and permeating global consciousness, she manages to keep all four feet—and often her nose—close to the ground. Tillie remains, in essence, an ordinary dog. One of her greatest gifts to humans is the opportunity for us to expand our notions of what an ordinary dog is capable of achieving. It is a lesson that might extend to other species as well, including our own. Thank you, Tillie.

2005 WORK

THE EYE OF FU MANCHU
(left)

Tillamook Cheddar, 2005
Oil stick on paper
20.5 x 14.5 inches
Collection of the Artist

ULTRAMARINE

Tillamook Cheddar,
  2004–2005
Oil stick on paper
14.5 x 20.5 inches
Collection of the Artist

TILLIE PIÑATA:

Mike Bilyk, 2004
Mixed Media
Dimensions variable
Private Collection

PART THREE:
CHECK THE TECHNIQUE
METHOD + MATERIALS

TILLIE'S
TECHNIQUE

Tillie's method today remains essentially the same as when she created her first carbon print, scratching away at that yellow legal pad when she was still a puppy. As her materials have evolved beyond the realm of office supplies, the artist has continued to hone her technique.

In her second material phase, Tillie worked on prefabricated color-transfer paper affixed to a mat board with a thorough coating of packing tape. I now prepare a specially layered recording device that allows her markings to be preserved in brilliant colors on paper of the highest archival quality. On a rigid base of mat or foam core supporting a sheet of lithograph paper, I place a paint-coated sheet of Denril vellum paper (paint-side down) with an insulating layer of clear Mylar on top.

Tillie's zest for art has not diminished over the years; nor has her astounding work ethic. She knows exactly what's in store whenever I set about preparing her materials, and she watches me with piqued interest until my prep work is complete. By the time her canvas is ready, she is literally trembling with anticipation.

The artist jumps up to snatch the wrapped package from my hands before I have a chance to place it on the floor. She attacks the outer surface of her work-in-progress with ecstatic aggression, applying pressure with teeth and claws in a methodic ritual marked by dramatic shifts in tempo and intensity. The resultant sharp and sweeping intersecting lines complement Tillie's delicate paw prints and subtle tongue impressions. The expressionistic image is never fully revealed on the paper beneath until she is finished and the outer layers are removed.

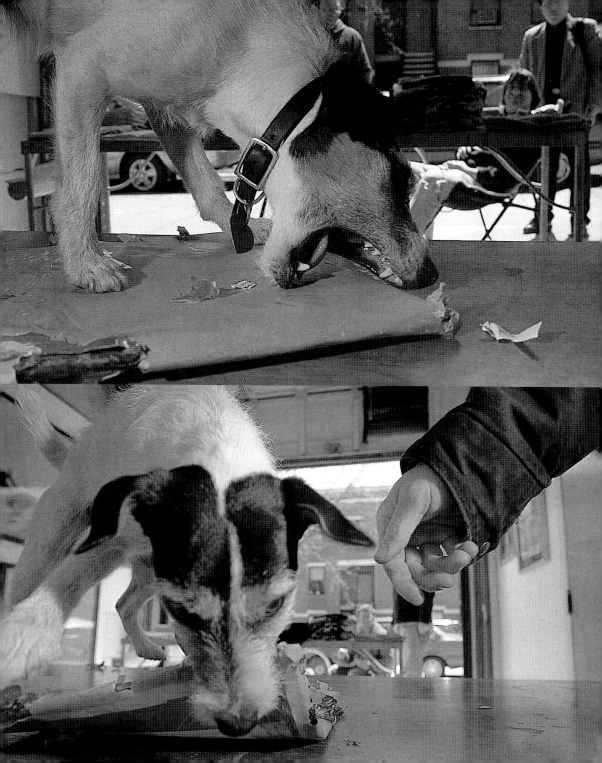

About the Author

F. Bowman Hastie III was born in Limestone,
Maine, and grew up eating Tillamook cheddar
cheese in Portland, Oregon. He now lives in Brooklyn, New York, with Tillamook Cheddar the dog,
and her son, Doc Chinook Strong-heart Cheddar.

PHOTO CREDITS

Cover photo by Dirk Westphal

Pages 2–3 photo by Dirk Westphal

Page 6 photo by Albert Delamour

Page 11 photo by Dirk Westphal

Page 13 photo by Claudette Beahrs

Page 16 photo by Albert Delamour

Page 19 photos by Albert Delamour

Page 24 photo by Dirk Westphal

Page 30 photo by Dirk Westphal

Page 37 photo by Dirk Westphal

Page 45 image by Diane Dwyer

Page 57 photo by Dirk Westphal

Page 65 photo by Albert Delamour

Page 72 photo by Dirk Westphal

Page 78 photo by Dirk Westphal

Page 79 photos by Dirk Westphal

Page 80 author photo by
 Albert Delamour

All other photos by
 F. Bowman Hastie III